DEADLY CREATURES

DEADLY REPTILES

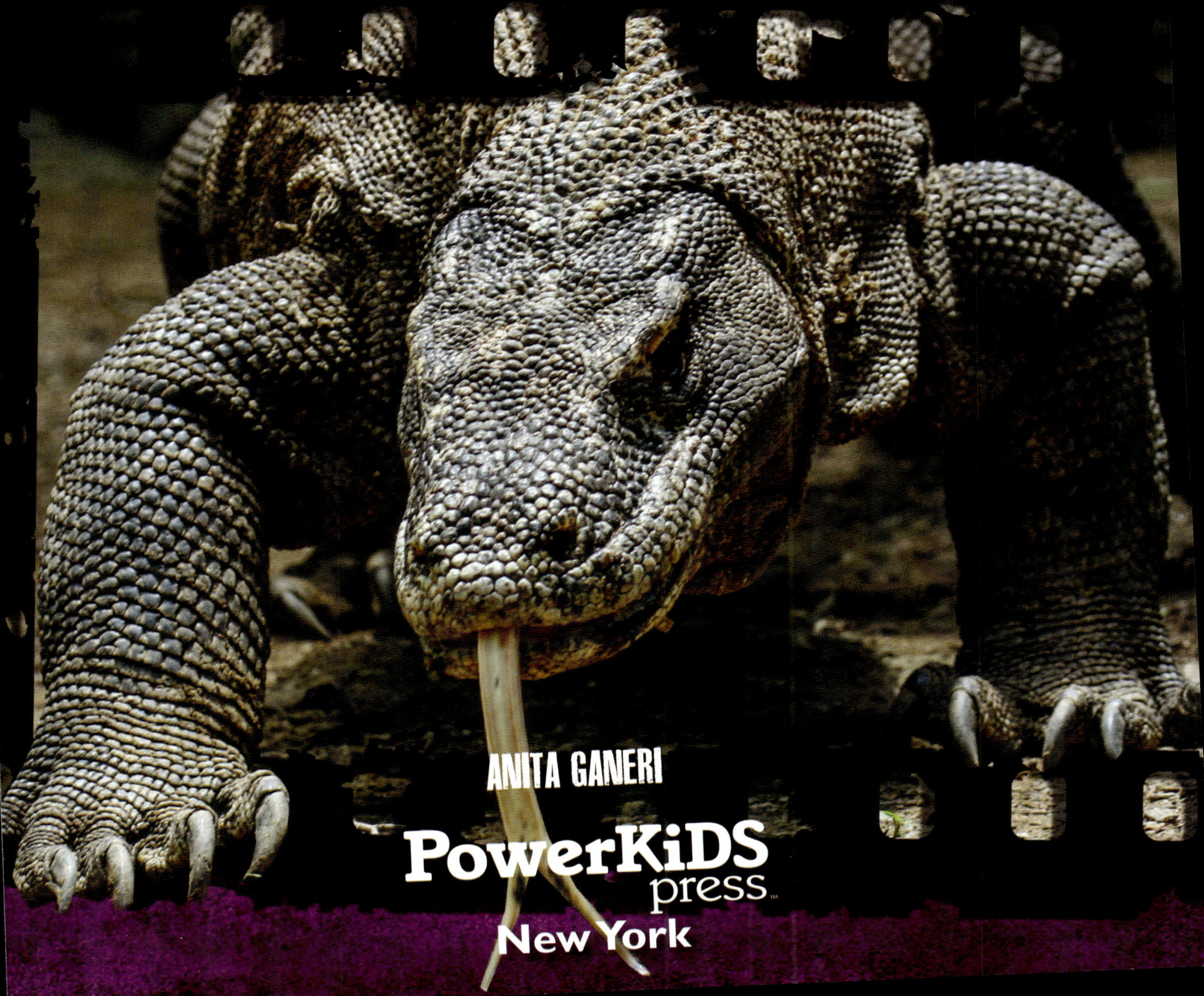

ANITA GANERI

PowerKiDS press
New York

Published in 2022 by The Rosen Publishing Group, Inc.
29 East 21st Street, New York, NY 10010

Originally Published in English by Haynes Publishing under the title: Deadly Creatures Pocket Manual © Haynes Publishing 2019

Cataloging-in-Publication Data
Names: Ganeri, Anita, 1961-.
Title: Deadly reptiles / Anita Ganeri.
Description: New York : PowerKids Press, 2022. | Series: Deadly creatures
Identifiers: ISBN 9781725331792 (pbk.) | ISBN 9781725331815 (library bound) | ISBN 9781725331808 (6 pack) | ISBN 9781725331822 (ebook)
Subjects: LCSH: Dangerous reptiles--Juvenile literature.
Classification: LCC QL645.7 G35 2022 | DDC 597.9165--dc23

Design: Richard Parsons

Photo Credits: Cover Kit Korzun/Shutterstock.com; pp. 5, 15, Alamy; p. 7 https://commons.wikimedia.org/wiki/File:Alligator_mississippiensis_01.JPG; pp. 9, 11, 13, 19, 29 iStock; p. 16. https://commons.wikimedia.org/wiki/File:Eunectes_murinus_(2).jpg; p. 23 PhotocechCZ/Shutterstock.com; p. 24 Walkabout Photo Guides/Shutterstock.com; p. 25 Sergey Uryadnikov/Shutterstock.com; p. 27 https://commons.wikimedia.org/wiki/File:Saltwater_Crocodile_on_a_river_bank.jpg; p. 28 https://commons.wikimedia.org/wiki/File:Crocodile_Crocodylus-porosus_amk2.jpg; p. 31 https://commons.wikimedia.org/wiki/File:Pelamis_platura,_Costa_Rica.jpg.

Manufactured in the United States of America

CPSIA Compliance Information: Batch #CSPK22. For Further Information contact Rosen Publishing, New York, New York at 1-800-237-9932.

CONTENTS

PYTHON SEBAE

AFRICAN ROCK PYTHON

Africa's largest snake, the African rock python has a massive muscular body and lives in a wide range of habitats. Because of its size, it spends most of its time on the ground, but it is also an excellent swimmer and will often ambush prey from the water's edge.

VITAL STATISTICS

BODY LENGTH:	up to 20 feet (6 m)
WEIGHT:	up to 250 lb (113 kg)
EATS:	monkeys, antelope, lizards, crocodiles
LIFE SPAN:	25 years
HABITAT:	savannas, rivers, forests
DISTRIBUTION:	

KILLER COILS

African rock pythons kill their prey by constriction. They normally hunt wild animals, although if they live close to humans they have been known to kill goats, chickens, dogs, and other domestic pets. A rock python hunts its prey at dusk, using its heat-sensing organs. It sits and waits until an animal comes close. Then it strikes, gripping its victim in its teeth and coiling its body around it. Every time its victim breathes out, the snake tightens its grip.

DID YOU KNOW?

Female African rock pythons are caring parents. The female lays her eggs in an empty burrow or termite mound. Then she coils around the eggs to protect them.

DEADLY FEATURES

With its huge body and powerful coils, this snake can constrict an animal as large as an antelope. It also has large, curved teeth and can give a very painful bite. It is known to be bad-tempered and will readily bite if provoked.

ALLIGATOR MISSISSIPPIENSIS

AMERICAN ALLIGATOR

Alligators can be told apart from crocodiles by their rounded snouts and their lower teeth that do not stick out when their mouths are closed. The American alligator lives in freshwater swamps, rivers, and lakes in the United States. It has a powerful, armor-plated body, with a long tail and webbed feet.

VITAL STATISTICS

BODY LENGTH:	8–11 feet (2.4–3.4 m)
WEIGHT:	up to 1,000 lb (450 kg)
EATS:	fish, mammals
LIFE SPAN:	35–50 years
HABITAT:	swamps, rivers, lakes
DISTRIBUTION:	

RIVER HUNTER

Lying in the water, the alligator looks like a floating log until its prey comes close. Young alligators start off by eating shrimp, snails, and insects, but adults hunt fish, frogs, snakes, and mammals. American alligators hunt mainly at night, snapping up prey in the water. They also catch animals that come to drink at the water's edge.

DID YOU KNOW?

In the dry season, alligators dig holes in the ground, using their snouts and tails. These "alligator holes" fill with water and make a welcome hiding place from the heat.

DEADLY FEATURES

An American alligator's huge jaws are lined with up to 80 sharp, conical teeth and it may have the strongest bite of any animal. It grabs its prey in a vicelike grip, then holds on to it until it drowns.

DENDROASPIS POLYLEPIS

BLACK MAMBA

One of the world's most venomous snakes, the black mamba lives in southern and eastern Africa. It is found in rocky hills or on the wooded savanna. It hides inside termite mounds and hollow trees or basks in the sun. It gets its name from the black coloring inside its mouth, though its skin is actually olive green or brownish-gray.

VITAL STATISTICS

BODY LENGTH:	8.2–13 feet (2.5–4 m)
WEIGHT:	3.3 lb (1.5 kg)
EATS:	rodents, small birds
LIFE SPAN:	12 years
HABITAT:	forests, grasslands
DISTRIBUTION:	

DEADLY STRIKE

From the same family as cobras, the black mamba is five times as venomous as a king cobra. It uses its poison to kill its prey of rodents and small birds. Usually shy and secretive, it can be particularly dangerous if it is cornered or threatened. Then it raises its head off the ground, opens its mouth wide and flicks out its tongue, and hisses before striking.

DID YOU KNOW?

The black mamba is the fastest-moving snake on land. At top speed, it can move at 12 miles (20 km) per hour for short bursts, especially if it is trying to avoid danger. It can also climb trees.

DEADLY FEATURES

A black mamba's venom is deadly. The snake strikes its prey several times at speed, then waits for it to become paralyzed and die before swallowing it whole. Its bite could kill a human being in 20 minutes, unless treated with antivenom.

CROTALUS ATROX

DIAMONDBACK RATTLESNAKE

The Western diamondback rattlesnake lives in the southwestern United States and parts of Mexico. It likes dry, rocky places where it can hide. It is well camouflaged by its yellowish-gray skin and is named after the dark diamond shapes running along its back.

VITAL STATISTICS

BODY LENGTH:	3–5 feet (0.9–1.5 m)
WEIGHT:	up to 15 lb (6.8 kg)
EATS:	birds, small mammals, lizards
LIFE SPAN:	15 years
HABITAT:	deserts, scrubland
DISTRIBUTION:	

DEADLY RATTLE

Rattlesnakes are famous for the scales at the end of their tails. They are made up of loosely attached hard plates of keratin, which is also what the hair and horns of other animals are made of. If a rattlesnake is threatened, it coils its body, ready to strike, and shakes its rattle at its attacker as a warning. The scales knock together when the tail is shaken, making an eerie, rattling sound. If its attacker is not frightened away, the snake strikes.

DID YOU KNOW?

Rattlesnakes have special heat-sensing pits on the sides of their heads that allow them to track down their prey in the dark.

DEADLY FEATURES

Rattlesnakes have long fangs and a deadly poisonous bite. They use their venom for self-defense and to catch prey. The venom kills an animal in seconds and also helps to digest its body.

BITIS GABONICA

GABOON VIPER

Found in the rain forests of Africa, gaboon vipers are the largest and heaviest vipers, growing up to 6.5 feet (2 m) long. Their skin is brownish-gray with striking patterns of yellow and black diamonds, triangles, and spots. These markings help to hide them as they lie among the leaves on the forest floor.

VITAL STATISTICS

BODY LENGTH:	up to 6.5 feet (2 m)
WEIGHT:	up to 22 lb (10 kg)
EATS:	rodents, birds, frogs, toads
LIFE SPAN:	18 years
HABITAT:	rain forests, grasslands
DISTRIBUTION:	

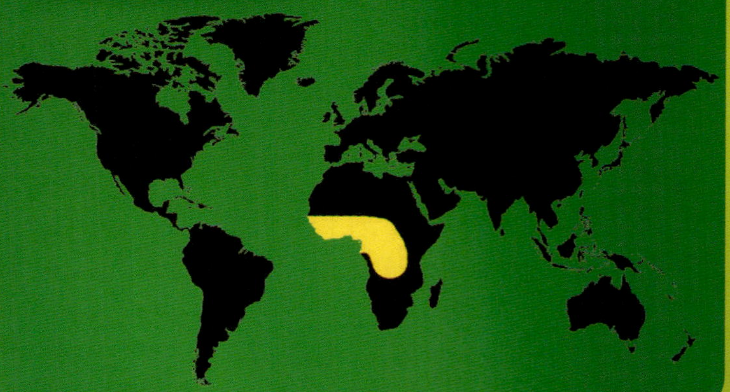

NIGHT HUNTERS

Gaboon vipers hunt alone and at night. They are most active at sunset when they start to search for their prey of rodents, birds, frogs, and toads. They usually lie among the leaves, waiting for prey to pass by. Then they attack with a deadly, venomous bite.

DEADLY FEATURES

The gaboon viper has the longest fangs of any venomous snake. Its fangs measure about 2 inches (5 cm) and inject large amounts of venom if they bite. To keep the fangs out of the way, they turn back into the mouth when the mouth is closed. When the mouth opens, the fangs flick out rapidly.

DID YOU KNOW?

Gaboon vipers can be deadly but they are usually very placid. If they are threatened, they hiss loudly but do not strike unless they are seriously provoked.

EUNECTES MURINUS

GREEN ANACONDA

The green anaconda is the world's largest snake. It can grow to more than 30 feet (9 m) in length and its stocky, muscular body is thicker than a human leg. Its skin is dark green, with a pattern of large, black spots. This provides the snake with camouflage both in the water and on the rain forest floor.

VITAL STATISTICS

BODY LENGTH:	up to 30 feet (9 m)
WEIGHT:	220–440 lb (100–200 kg)
EATS:	fish, birds, tapirs, caimans, deer
LIFE SPAN:	up to 10 years
HABITAT:	rain forest rivers

DISTRIBUTION:

SWIMMING SKILLS

Anacondas spend most of their time in the water, where they hunt for prey. They live mostly in shallow, slow-moving rain forest rivers and swamps in South America. They are superbly adapted for life in the water. Their eyes and nostrils are on top of their heads so that they can still see and breathe even when they are swimming or lying half submerged in the water. Young anacondas are born in the water, and can swim right away.

DID YOU KNOW?

Anacondas' upper and lower jaws are connected by ligaments that are very stretchy, like elastic. This allows them to open their mouths wide enough to swallow prey many times as wide as their heads.

SNAKE PRINTS

The pattern of scales on the underside of an anaconda's tail is different in each snake. It can be used to identify individual snakes, just as fingerprints can in humans.

STEALTHY HUNTER

An anaconda hunts for its prey at night. It mainly eats fish, frogs, birds, and sometimes larger animals such as deer, caimans, and capybaras. It lies in the water, with just its snout showing. When prey comes near or stops at the water's edge to drink, the anaconda swims quickly towards it. It grabs the prey in its jaws, coils around the animal, then squeezes until its victim suffocates. Then it swallows the prey whole, head first. Anacondas occasionally hunt on land, although they move much more sluggishly. Smaller, younger anacondas have been found resting in trees, but fully grown female anacondas are much too heavy to climb.

Local names for anacondas are **BULL KILLERS** and **ELEPHANT KILLERS** because of their huge size.

DEADLY FEATURES

Anacondas are not venomous. They belong to a group of snakes called boas, which kill their prey by constriction (squeezing). Wrapped in an anaconda's massive coils, prey does not stand a chance and eventually stops breathing.

DID YOU KNOW?

It takes an anaconda a long time to digest its food. After a big meal, it may not need to eat again for weeks or even months.

OPHIOPHAGUS HANNAH

KING COBRA

The world's longest venomous snake, the king cobra lives in India and parts of Southeast Asia. It is found near streams in rain forests and mangrove swamps, where it spends the day hunting for its prey of other snakes and lizards. It locates its prey by smell and sight, then chases after it and strikes.

VITAL STATISTICS

BODY LENGTH:	10–18 feet (3–5.4 m)
WEIGHT:	13 lb (6 kg)
EATS:	other snakes, lizards
LIFE SPAN:	20 years
HABITAT:	rain forests, mangrove swamps
DISTRIBUTION:	

SNAKE SKIN

A king cobra is a powerfully built snake, reaching about 18 feet (5.4 m) in length. Adults have greenish-brown and black skin with yellow or white markings and a cream or pale yellow belly. Young cobras are black with yellow bands. Even though it is a large snake, a king cobra is remarkably fast-moving and agile.

UNDER THREAT?

Although not officially endangered, king cobras are under threat from destruction of their habitat. They are also hunted and killed by people who are afraid of them and who also use their skin, meat, and bile for traditional medicine.

DID YOU KNOW?

When threatened, a king cobra lifts its body off the ground to a height of about 5 feet (1.5 m). Then it spreads out its hood like a fan and growls!

The king cobra's Latin/scientific name means SNAKE EATER, after its favorite prey.

EGGS AND YOUNG

A female cobra is particularly deadly when she is guarding her nest. King cobras are caring parents, making complex nests from piles of leaves, grass, and soil. The female then makes a hole in the top, lays 20 to 40 eggs, and covers them with leaves. She sits on top and guards the nest fiercely until the eggs hatch. The male also stays nearby. Baby cobras can already bite as soon as they hatch.

DID YOU KNOW?

Unlike most snakes, the king cobra does not make a hissing sound when it is threatened. Instead, it makes a deep growling noise from its throat.

DEADLY FEATURES

A king cobra has two short, fixed fangs at the front of its mouth. These inject venom, made in its salivary glands, into its prey. It can produce enough poison in a single bite to kill 20 to 30 adult humans or an adult Asian elephant.

VARANUS KOMODOENSIS

KOMODO DRAGON

The mighty Komodo dragon is the largest lizard in the world. Growing up to 10 feet (3 m) long, it has a heavy, stocky body with short, strong legs and a long, muscular tail. It is very rare and is found only on the island of Komodo and a few other islands in Indonesia.

VITAL STATISTICS

BODY LENGTH:	up to 10 feet (3 m)
WEIGHT:	150–360 lb (68–163 kg)
EATS:	carrion, deer, wild pigs, birds
LIFE SPAN:	30–50 years
HABITAT:	grasslands
DISTRIBUTION:	

DRAGON DIET

Komodo dragons mainly eat carrion, but they are also ferocious hunters, ambushing large animals such as deer, goats, and wild pigs. They grab their prey in their sharp claws, then give a lethal bite to the underside or throat. They follow the injured animal until it dies, and tear it apart with their sharp, serrated teeth.

DEADLY RATING

DID YOU KNOW?

Young Komodo dragons spend their first few months living high up in the trees to avoid falling prey to predators, including cannibalistic adults.

Many of the world's Komodo dragons live in Komodo National Park.

DEADLY FEATURES

A Komodo dragon's saliva contains more than 50 different kinds of lethal bacteria. These are injected into prey as the dragon bites. This causes deadly infections and eventually death.

CROCODYLUS POROSUS

SALTWATER CROCODILE

The saltwater crocodile is enormous. Growing up to more than 20 feet (6 m) in length, it is the largest crocodile and also the largest reptile in the world. It lives in rivers and along coasts in Southeast Asia, Australia, and around the Pacific Ocean. This giant is superbly adapted for hunting its prey in the water, with a powerful tail, webbed back feet, and crushing jaws.

VITAL STATISTICS

BODY LENGTH:	up to 22 feet (7 m)
WEIGHT:	880–2,200 lb (400–1,000 kg)
EATS:	birds, mammals, reptiles, fish, crabs
LIFE SPAN:	over 60 years
HABITAT:	rivers, coasts

DISTRIBUTION:

KILLER CROC

A saltwater crocodile is a carnivore, feeding on birds, mammals, and reptiles. It lies almost completely submerged in the water, hiding from its prey. Its eyes, ears, and nostrils are on top of its head so that it can still see, hear, and breathe. It can also block off its throat so that it can open its mouth underwater without drowning. When its prey gets near, it lunges out of the water, grabs it, and drags it underwater to eat.

DID YOU KNOW?

Saltwater crocodiles have been hunted for their meat, eggs, and skin, and also threatened by the loss of their habitats. In Australia, some are taken from the wild and moved to farms for breeding.

CROC TALK

To communicate with each other, saltwater crocodiles use a series of barking calls. Hatchlings give a short, high bark. Adults hiss or cough if they feel threatened and give a long, low growl to attract mates.

NESTS AND BABIES

A female saltwater crocodile lays her 40 to 60 eggs in a mounded nest made from mud and plants and built close to the water. She guards the nest fiercely for three months until the eggs hatch. As soon as she hears the newly hatched crocodiles chirping, she digs them out of the nest and carries them to water in her mouth so that they can learn to swim.

A group of saltwater crocodiles is known as a BASK (on land) and a FLOAT (in the water).

DID YOU KNOW?

Saltwater crocodiles are very strong swimmers. They sometimes travel long distances out to sea and have been found over 600 miles (965 km) from land.

DEADLY FEATURES

A saltwater crocodile's sheer size makes it a deadly predator. It is strong enough to drag a fully grown water buffalo into the water. Its powerful jaws can snap shut with massive force, and are lined with 60 or more sharp teeth.

PELAMIS PLATURUS
YELLOW-BELLIED SEA SNAKE

The deadliest snakes in the world are found in the warm waters of the Indian and Pacific Oceans. They are superbly adapted to life in the sea. They use their flattened tails as paddles for swimming and can stay underwater for 30 minutes to two hours at a time, closing their nostrils to keep water out.

VITAL STATISTICS

BODY LENGTH:	up to 5 feet (1.5 m)
WEIGHT:	3.3 lb (1.5 kg)
EATS:	fish, fish eggs, mollusks, crustaceans
LIFE SPAN:	4–5 years
HABITAT:	tropical coastal waters

DISTRIBUTION:

SHY SNAKES

Sea snakes forage for food during the day. Their main prey is fish (particularly eels and fish eggs), mollusks, and crustaceans. On coral reefs, they use their small heads to pull eels from the sandy seabed. Sea snakes use a poisonous bite to kill their prey. They also use their venom in self-defense, although they are usually shy and only bite if provoked.

DID YOU KNOW?

Sea snakes sometimes gather in huge groups, thousands strong. It is thought that they do this to breed. After storms, large numbers may be washed up on the beach.

DEADLY FEATURES

Most sea snakes are deadly. The yellow-bellied sea snake's venom is 10 times stronger than a cobra's. But the snakes have tiny fangs and only inject small amounts of venom in each bite.

GLOSSARY

camouflage to blend into surroundings
carrion the bodies of dead animals
constriction making something smaller and tighter
endangered in danger of dying out
fangs long, sharp teeth
habitat the natural place where an animal lives
hatch to come out of an egg
jaws the bones in the head that hold the teeth
paralyzed to be unable to move parts of the body
savanna a large, flat grassland with few trees
serrated having a row of small points along the side, like a saw

INDEX